ZONDERVAN

A Savior is Born: Rocks Tell the Story of Christmas
Copyright © 2018 by Patti Rokus

Photos © 2018 Patti Rokus

This title is also available as a Zondervan ebook.

Requests for information should be addressed to:
Zondervan, 3900 Sparks Dr. SE, Grand Rapids, Michigan 49546

ISBN 978-0-310-76496-0

Interior design: Patti Rokus

Printed in Vietnam

23 24 25 DSC 10 9 8 7 6 5

Rocks Tell
the Story of Christmas

A Savior is Born

Some of the
greatest stories
in the world are true.

This is one of them.

Mary, you're going to have a baby!

—Luke 1:28-38

Waiting for Jesus.

To Bethlehem.

—Luke 2:1-4

In a lowly stable.

Lamb of God.

–Luke 2:6–7

—Luke 2:8-12

Tidings of great joy.

Glory to God.

—Luke 2:13-14

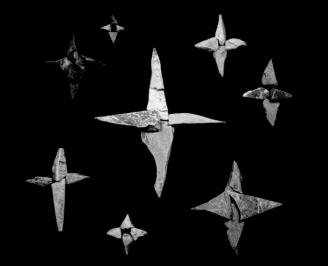

Let's go see.

—Luke 2:15

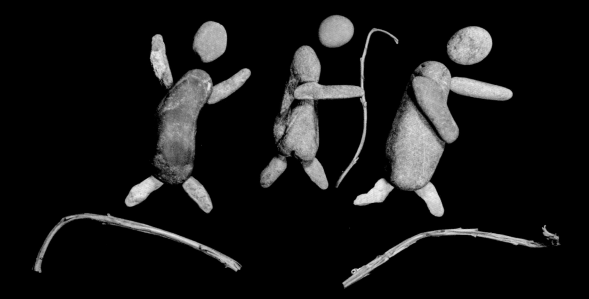

Rejoice!

—Luke 2:16-17

King of Kings!

—Matthew 2:10-11

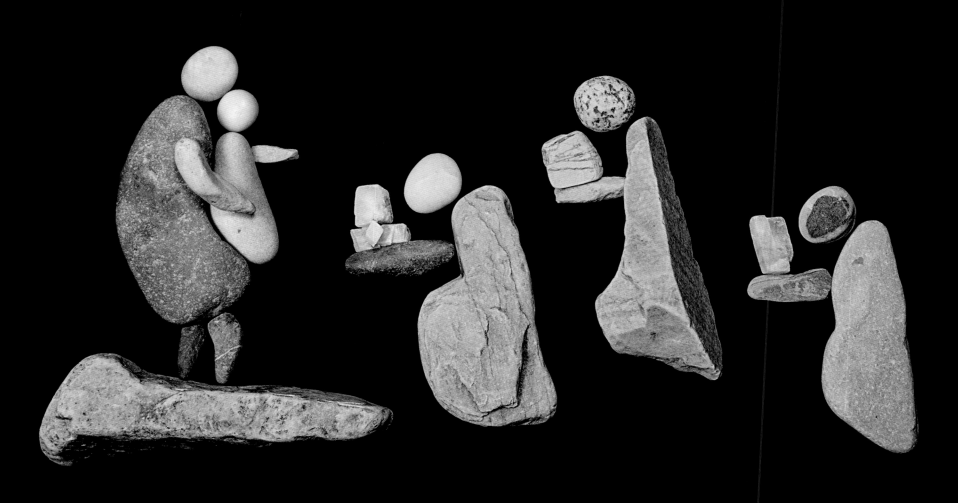

God so loved the world that He gave His only begotten Son.

—John 3:16

Now it's your turn.
What will you create
with rocks?

Note from the author

Each one of these rocks called out to me as I hiked through the forests and streams of the Pacific Northwest during a solo camping trip. I couldn't resist holding each one, and soon my pockets were heavy with treasures that eventually filled my bucket. I didn't know why I felt so compelled to take them home, but I did feel like a child again, reveling in the beauty of simple things.

Finishing my trip with a visit to Mom's house, free from the regular routine of life, I indulged in a morning of no expectations, and quiet, childlike wonder as I dumped out my bucket of rocks on Mom's back porch and mindlessly pushed them around. One rock looked distinctly like someone kneeling, so I put a round rock above it as a head—and saw Mary bowing before an angel.

Surprised by this obvious likeness, I wondered what an angel would look like as an ordinary rock, and there in the pile it emerged. With six simple rocks, a miracle shined through. I ran upstairs to find Mom and showed her my discovery. We spent the morning together moving rocks around until we found the entire Christmas story in that one bucket of rocks.

I wondered if each rock was shaped over time for this very moment—to represent Mary or Joseph, an angel, or even our Savior. Jesus Himself told the Pharisees that if His disciples "should hold their peace, the stones would immediately cry out" (Luke 19:40) to testify of Him. And so they do in this book and in all of nature.

Could it be that we're like that too—designed for significance that we cannot begin to imagine, and that will inevitably be so, not by our own making, but by a power much greater and more loving than we ever imagined?

Nature with all her beauty, diversity, and majesty will always be an important source of my connection to God. I start feeling small and disconnected when I'm too long from a walk in the woods. The wonder I feel among the trees and the earth cannot be explained and is reserved only for the soul who steps foot and heart onto her ground. Anyone can share in the abundance of the outdoors and be filled up with the peace and contentment of becoming part of her grandeur.

Let us bring our children to their spiritual roots and reintroduce them to their connection to all things—especially to God. We might be surprised what they will teach us when they rediscover that all things testify of Jesus Christ, and why.

Please visit my website, **RocksTellStories.com**, and share your own pictures of rocks telling stories.

LUKE 1:28–38 (NKJV)

And the angel said to her, "Rejoice, highly favored *one,* the Lord *is* with you; blessed *are* you among women!"

Then the angel said, "Do not be afraid, Mary, for you have found favor with God. And behold, you will conceive and bring forth a Son, and shall call His name Jesus. He will be great, and will be called the Son of the Highest; and the Lord God will give Him the throne of His father David. And He will reign over the house of Jacob forever, and of His kingdom there will be no end."

Then Mary said to the angel, "How can this be, since I do not know a man?"

And the angel answered and said to her, "*The* Holy Spirit will come upon you, and the power of the Highest will overshadow you; therefore, also, that Holy One who is to be born will be called the Son of God. For with God nothing will be impossible."

Then Mary said, "Behold the maidservant of the Lord! Let it be to me according to your word."

LUKE 2:1–17 (NKJV)

And it came to pass in those days *that* a decree went out from Caesar Augustus that all the world should be registered. So all went to be registered, everyone to his own city.

Joseph went up from Galilee to the city of David, which is called Bethlehem, to be registered with Mary, his betrothed wife, who was with child. So it was, that while they were there, the days were completed for her to be delivered. And she brought forth her firstborn Son, and wrapped Him in swaddling cloths, and laid Him in a manger, because there was no room for them in the inn.

Now there were in the same country shepherds living out in the fields, keeping watch over their flock by night. And behold, an angel of the Lord stood before them, and the glory of the Lord shone around them, and they were greatly afraid. Then the angel said to them, "Do not be afraid, for behold, I bring you good tidings of great joy which will be to all people. For there is born to you this day in the city of David a Savior, who is Christ the Lord. And this *will be* the sign to you: You will find a Babe wrapped in swaddling cloths, lying in a manger."

MATTHEW 2:10–11 (NKJV)

When [the Wise Men] saw the star, they rejoiced with great joy. And when they had come into the house, they saw the young Child with Mary His mother, and fell down and worshiped Him. And when they had opened their treasures, they presented gifts to Him: gold, frankincense, and myrrh.